HARVARD
UNIVERSITY

CRESCENT BOOKS
NEW YORK

CLB 1533
© 1987 Colour Library Books Ltd., Guildford, Surrey, England.
Printed and bound in Barcelona, Spain by Cronion, S.A.
All rights reserved.
1987 edition published by Crescent Books, distributed by Crown Publishers, Inc.
ISBN 0 517 61897 4
h g f e d c b a

Veritas is the Latin word for "truth." At Harvard, it sums up a way of life. It began back in 1636, only 16 years after the Pilgrims landed at Plymouth Rock. The original idea of the college's Puritan founders was to educate their own ministers following the pattern of English universities, but adding touches of what they perceived to be the true light. It soon became apparent that the new country had other important needs beyond the ecclesiastical, and Harvard marched to the forefront by broadening its curriculum to include the sciences, law and the arts. In the process it became influential in the political and social structure of England's colonies in America.

Harvard, which had used an English system as its model, became the model for other colleges established in the Colonies, and the quest for truth that exists on campuses from coast to coast even today still looks to Harvard for its inspiration.

By the time the Revolution was fought, after eight Harvard men, including John Hancock, had signed a Declaration of Independence, there were nine colleges in America and they were beginning to be thought of as a means for young men to advance themselves. Harvard was still the inspiration. And for 350 years its alumnae have seemed determined to prove the point. Harvard has produced six presidents, from John Adams to John F. Kennedy. It has produced Supreme Court Justices, cabinet members and just about every other kind of influential government official you care to name. But a Harvard diploma isn't always a ticket to Washington, D.C. The Harvard Business School is famous for the number of chief executive officers it has given corporate America. The Harvard Medical School has educated the deans of 36 other American medical schools. Harvard faculty members have won 29 Nobel Prizes, 25 of which were for science and medicine. The faculty of Arts and Sciences has earned 25 Pulitzer Prizes.

All of that is truth and all of it well-known. But possibly because of it, there is a myth about Harvard that all of its students come from families with plenty of money and lots of influence, and that if a young person isn't a graduate of a prestigious prep school there is no point in applying to become an undergraduate at Harvard.

But consider the class of 1980: a big sixty-four percent of them came from public high schools. Are they from wealthy families? Sixty-six percent of the students enrolled at Harvard in 1986 received some form of financial aid. The Harvard admissions office is completely "needs-blind," and if a student is qualified they are prepared to help.

They screen more than 13,000 applications each year to find 2,184 freshmen. Of the ones they select, a big seventy-three percent, far and away the largest percentage of any American University, accept the bid. And why not? The prestige of Harvard University stays with every graduate for a lifetime. It can mean higher income and increased power, more respect and greater influence in any field. But it isn't something one gets by simply enrolling there. Of the many words of wisdom chiseled in stone on the walls of Harvard's buildings, the ones that sum up what Harvard expects of every student are: "Enter to grow in wisdom. Depart to serve better thy country and thy kind."

Harvard students have been taking that advice for more than 350 years, with the result that the influence of their school has kept growing and the influence of their school ties has kept improving. The University began as the first in the nation, and through the years has stayed number one in a country where higher education has become so important that there are now more than 2,000 colleges and universities in America, compared to 300 a century ago.

A century ago, when Harvard was marking its 250th anniversary, President Charles William Eliot said that universities "bring a portion of each successive generation to the confines of knowledge, to the very edge of the territory already conquered, and say to the eager youth: 'Thus far came our fathers. Now press you on!'" And as we press on, a single word still guides the destiny of Fair Harvard: Truth.

Facing page: the turquoise dome of Eliot House rises 230 feet above the Charles River.

A Harvard doctor's gown (top left) is earned at places like the Science Center (top right and above) or the Law School's Langdell Hall (facing page top), behind Louise Nevelson's *Night Wall I*. Henry Moore's *Four Piece Reclining Figure* (facing page bottom) is perfect for outdoor discussion. Indoor resources include Tibetan manuscripts at the Yenching Library (right).

4

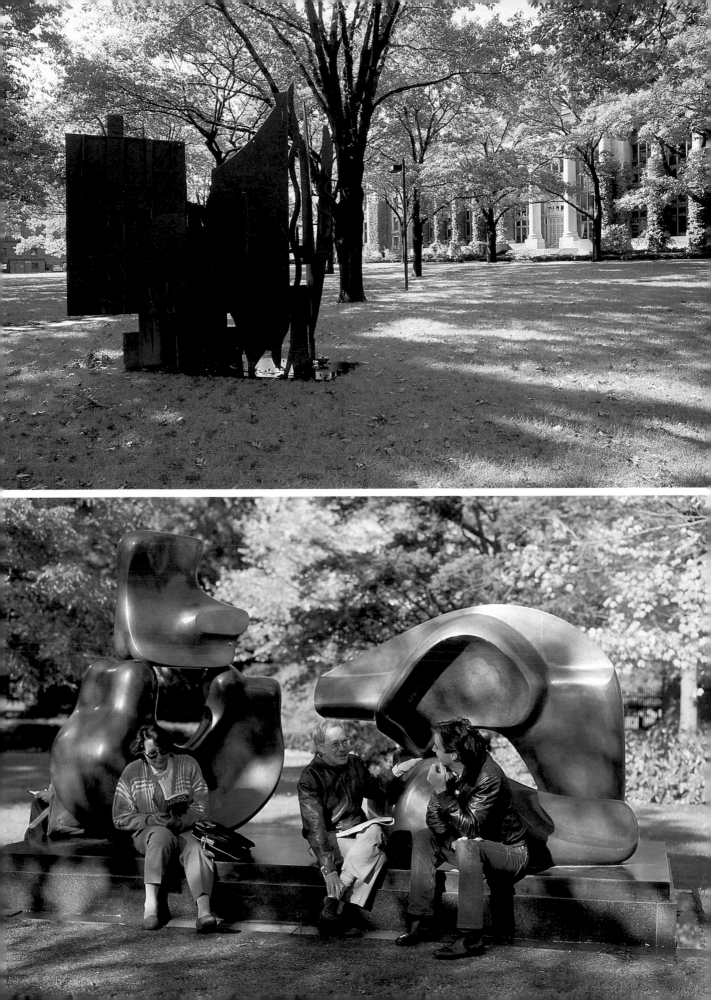

Houghton Library's Richardson Room (top), the
Kirkland House Library (facing page top), the Fogg
Museum's Naumberg Room (facing page bottom),
and the President's House (right) all provide quiet
retreats. But some rooms get crowded, as was the
case when Nobel Laureate Dudley Herschbach was
interviewed at the Mallinkrodt Laboratories (above).

Eliot House (facing page) is named for President
Charles Eliot, whose portrait by John Singer
Sargent hangs in its dining hall. The Church of the
New Jerusalem (above), though not a Harvard
building, was designed by Professor Herbert L.

Warren, first lecturer of Harvard's School of
Architecture. The Faculty Room in University Hall
(overleaf) contains portraits and busts of many
faculty members, a community that includes 29
Nobel Laureates.

The wide variety of architectural styles at Harvard includes University Hall (top), Littauer Center (facing page top), Fogg Art Museum (facing page bottom), Memorial Hall (right) and the Agassiz Theater in Radcliffe Yard (above and overleaf).

An air of peace and quiet dominates Harvard Yard
(top) and the Eliot House Courtyard (remaining
pictures these pages). Overleaf: there is usually
plenty of activity, however, at the Bright Hockey
Center (top left), the Blodgett Pool (top right),
Gordon Track and Tennis Center (bottom right)
and the Briggs Athletic Center (bottom left).

The Neo-Georgian President's House (above) was designed by Guy Lowell in 1912, three years after President Charles W. Eliot (facing page) retired as Harvard President. In the aerial view (overleaf) the building at the left front is the John F. Kennedy School of Government. The area between it and the Charles River is now Kennedy Memorial Park. The boathouse on the right is the Weld Boathouse. Eliot House is just behind it.

Widener Library (above, left and top) houses about a third of the university's collection, the largest in the world. Fogg Art Museum (facing page) has one of America's best collections of fine art. Overleaf: the Harry Elkins Widener Memorial Room in the museum is a work of art in itself.

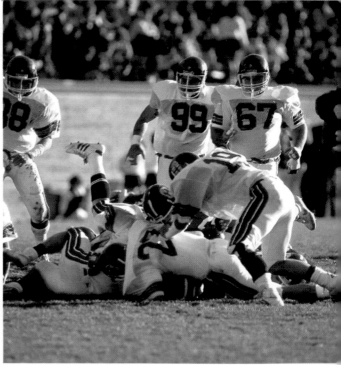

Harvard Stadium (these pages and overleaf), across the Charles River, seats 38,000 people and is the oldest college stadium in the country. When a game is scheduled, thousands cross Anderson Bridge to watch the team, hear the band and follow the cues of the cheerleaders.

These pages and overleaf: recollections of the day the Harvard Crimson met the Bruins from Brown at Harvard Stadium. Both teams compete in the Ivy League, whose name comes from the fact that it began with four colleges and used the Roman numeral designation "IV."

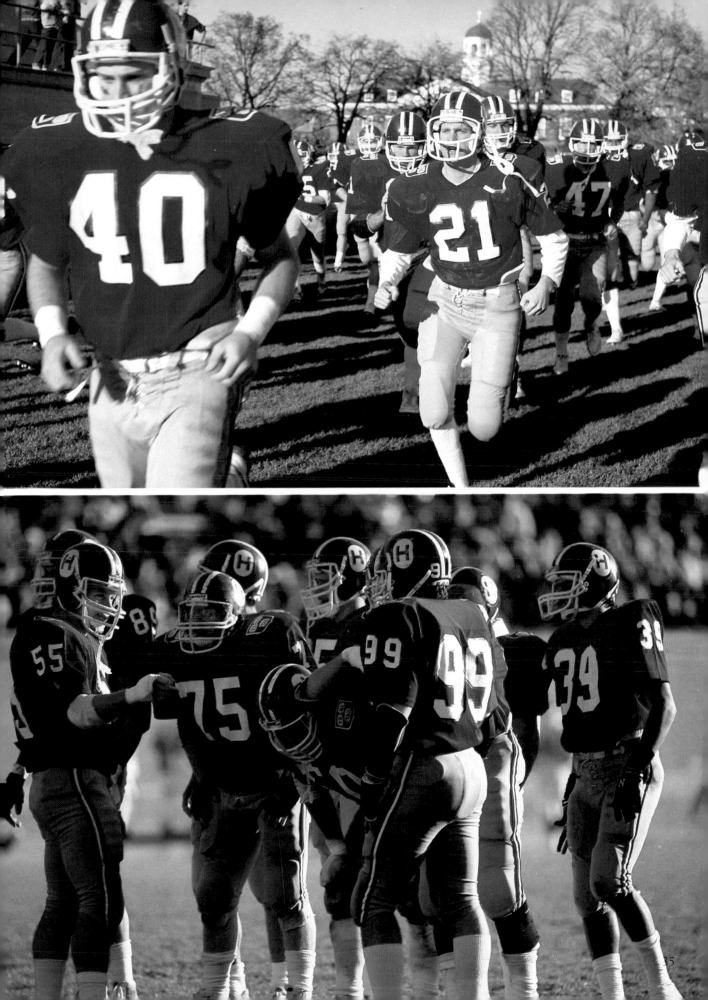

Kirkland House and its courtyard (facing page top) were named for a 19th-century Harvard president, John T. Kirkland. Langdell Hall of the Law School (facing page bottom) is one of seven professional libraries on campus. Busch-Reisinger Museum (above) has a collection of Northern European art. Overleaf: the kiosk on Harvard Square, in the shadow of Lehman Hall, keeps students in touch with events in the rest of the world.

The Busch-Reisinger Museum (above) was built in 1902 to house a gift of art treasures from Prussia. The Class of 1890 made a gift of this wonderful gate (facing page top) to Harvard Yard. The President's House at 17 Quincy Street (facing page bottom) was first used by President Abbott Lawrence Lowell. Rowing on the Charles River (overleaf) is a classic Harvard scene beneath the tower and chimneys of Dunster House and the modern, high-rise Mather House.

Dancers at Malkin Athletic Center (top) overlook the swimming pool (facing page top). The Science Center's lecture halls (above) are modern, but it also has a collection of antique equipment (right). The larger telescope (facing page bottom) is part of the Harvard Observatory, and students can read all about it in the Widener Library Reading Room 44 (overleaf).

Eliot Courtyard (above) was built as a memorial to his predecessor by President Lowell, whose own memorial (overleaf right) is also a landmark. Fay House (facing page) is a landmark at Radcliffe College, which was a separate, but equal, school for women from 1879 until 1973, when Harvard became coeducational. The view (overleaf left) across the rooftops didn't change at all.

Widener Library (top) serenely stands guard over
Harvard Yard (right), a short bicycle ride from the
freshman dormitories (above), past the the equally
serene statue (facing page) of John Harvard, a
product of the artistry of sculptor Daniel Chester
French.

Above: Henry Moore's *Four Piece Reclining Figure* is part of the modern art collection of the Massachusetts Institute of Technology. Quincy House Library (facing page), built in 1958, is a modern pavilion on stilts, and is a marked contrast to the more traditional Dunster House Library (overleaf), built in 1930.

The Soldiers' Monument (top) was placed on the Common in 1870. The Sackler Museum (above) was built in 1985 and the Harvard-Radcliffe Science Center (right, facing page top and overleaf) was added in 1972. In 1986, tents (facing page bottom) added their bright color to Harvard's 350th Anniversary celebrations.

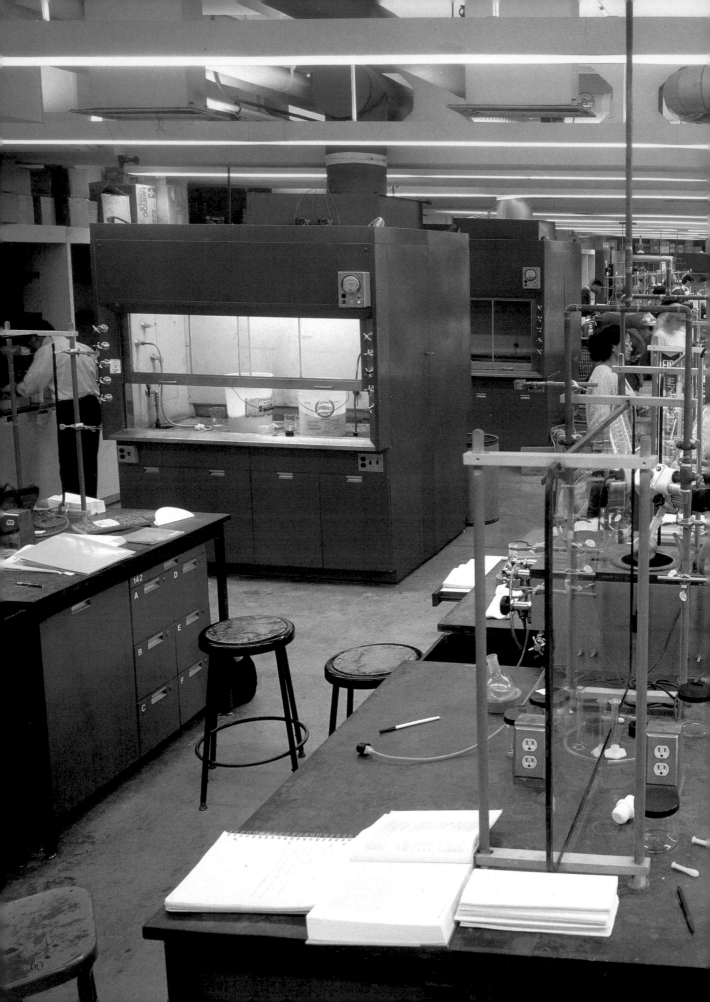

Smith Halls (above) is part of Kirkland House. Lowell House (facing page) has a carillon of 17 bells from a monastery in Moscow. Harvard Hall (overleaf), built in 1776, was used as a dining hall by George Washington and his troops, who were billeted in nearby buildings during the Revolutionary War.